THE MANAGER'S KITBAG

Tony Kemmer

Illustrations by Frid

2000

First published in 2007 by Management Books 2000 Ltd
Forge House, Limes Road
Kemble, Cirencester
Gloucestershire, GL7 6AD, UK
Tel: 0044 (0) 1285 771441
Fax: 0044 (0) 1285 771055
E-mail: info@mb2000.com
Web: www.mb2000.com

British Library Cataloguing in Publication Data is available

ISBN 9781852525569

ᑐᐁ**R'S KITBAG**

012

Barking	8724 8725	**Thames View**	8270 4164
Fanshawe	8270 4244	**Valence**	8270 6864
Marks Gate	8270 4165	**Wantz**	8270 4169
Markyate	8270 4137	**Robert Jeyes**	8270 4305
Rectory	8270 6233	**Castle Green**	8270 4166
Rush Green	8270 4304		

For a complete list of Management Books 2000 titles

visit our website on http://www.mb2000.com

Contents

Preface

After 30 years of learning about management 'the hard way', I thought I should write down what I've picked up on the journey. Hence this book.

If there is a theme, it is 'managing with people firmly at the front of mind' or, more briefly, 'people-centred management'. This is what I have tried to do throughout my working life and, in general, the approach has proved successful, though not always easy.

I would hope that very little of what I've written is glaringly obvious and that there's plenty to make you think. The idea is to dip in, read a page or two, reflect on what you've read and perhaps scribble yourself a reminder note in the margin (much to the horror of my publisher!)

This is definitely *not* a comprehensive 'how to manage' book. It's simply a collection of insights and ideas which hopefully will give you a new slant on old problems. I don't recommend fast skimming – if you try to read it from cover to cover you'll just get a sore head.

In conclusion can I say that I'm hugely grateful to my cartoonist, Fred Higton, who has done a tremendous job in bringing the text to life and injecting lots of humour. Can I also thank my family and, in particular, my wife Sue, who has had to put up with endless requests for comments and criticisms and long absences in the study.

Have fun!

Part 1

Thinking/Problem-Solving

Communication drives clarity

'Think more clearly, boy!' The stentorian tones of my school maths master still ring in my ears forty years later. Yet the injunction still rings true – with the increasingly complex environment in which we operate, never was clear thinking so important.

There are plenty of books offering advice on thinking techniques, but I suspect that most of us have our own private approaches that work most of the time – when we give ourselves the time, that is.

Over the years I've discovered that my best thinking comes from having to communicate my thoughts to others, usually through a presentation. Having twenty minutes to speak, eight slides to present and 3 bullet points per slide puts huge pressure on clarity. Suddenly that murky mess of ideas needs to be structured, sequenced and prioritised, and surprise, surprise, in the process new insights often emerge.

Report writing can have the same effect. Here I follow the suggestion from an ex-boss who said that the very first thing to do when starting a project is write the chapter headings of the final report and construct the project plan around that.

There are those who say that excessive simplification trivialises – the 'tabloid effect'. My response would be to look at the greatest historical thinkers, whether they be philosophers, scientists or religious leaders – almost invariably they were good communicators, and I suspect their communication actually enhanced the quality of their own thinking.

Long lists and short lists

There is something infinitely depressing about long lists particularly when these appear in serious documents. Whether it's a list of issues, observations, recommendations or whatever, I find myself asking "out of this lot, what's important, what comes before what, what depends on what?" I then wonder why the writer has made me do the work that he or she should have done.

As a means of communicating ideas, long lists can be disastrous as they complicate, confuse and frequently alienate the reader or listener.

So here you are trying to compose a report on issues found when touring the warehouse last week. How do you produce a short list from dozens of unrelated thoughts? I suggest asking the following questions:

1. Can the issues be grouped into a small number of different types?

2. Which are the biggest issues which if solved would make the biggest difference? (the 80/20 rule)

3. Which issues precede which? (i.e. which are root causes of others?) This will help with the sequence.

4. Are there some minor issues which can be bunched together under a 'miscellaneous' heading?

A small amount of time spent organising your thinking like this can vastly simplify the task of explaining to others. The Lord managed with only ten commandments – why can't you?

Hitting from different directions

Never trust a thinker with a tidy desk – good thinking is a messy business. However neat a report, if it's any good, I'll wager that the writer went through all sorts of chaos to get there – that's what deep thinking involves.

Over the years I've reluctantly come to the conclusion that when a question is really tough the only approach is to hit it from several different directions and hope that eventually things 'converge' on one answer. This applies whether you're trying to get to the bottom of some deep issue or equally when the aim is to formulate a neat way forward.

Imagine you're a consumer product manager and that new range which everyone said would be a stunning success bombs out in spite of all indications to the contrary. If you're a numbers person you'll pour over the figures in huge detail convinced that the reason for the failure is there somewhere. If you're an operational person you'll talk to all the sales people involved and see if a common picture emerges. If you're an ideas person you'll try to put yourself in the customer's shoes to work out what's going on. The fact is that all three approaches and more may be necessary.

As we all know, life's problems rarely have simple causes and effects. We are deluding ourselves if we think that somehow the world of work is simpler – it can't be because people are involved. Accept the fact that things are complicated and tell your PA or partner that for the next week or so a messy desk is inevitable

Levels of granularity

In our fast moving world efficient thinking and efficient communication of one's thoughts is increasingly important. This applies whether we are analysing problems, devising solutions or even when we're creating new concepts.

A useful question to ask yourself before plunging in to a new piece of thinking is "How much detail does this require?" It can be hugely beneficial both in terms of the quality of the finished output and the time and effort involved to consider up front the 'level of granularity' really needed.

So how might this work?

1. Monday morning the boss walks in and says "We've got a problem in the factory. Productivity is dropping but the other measures look OK. Find out what's happening. Report with recommendations on my desk this Friday!"

2. Instinct tells you to rush off and start talking to people – anyone who can help. Within two days you've got mounds of meeting notes, reams of printouts and not a clue how to bash this into something meaningful by the end of the week.

3. An alternative approach is to stop and consider what is wanted. Where are things likely to be going wrong? What are the likely causes? What sort of recommendations is the boss expecting? From that you can then work out in how much detail you actually need to analyse the problem and formulate a solution.

4. Sorting out the necessary level of granularity before you start thinking is a great saver of time and sanity.

Part 2

People Management

Everyone's unique value

Having worked with hundreds of people over the last 30 years I cannot recall having come upon anyone who in the right environment, with the right direction and the right support could not make a valuable and moreover a uniquely valuable contribution to the task at hand.

Sometimes it's a unique combination of skills, sometimes a unique set of experiences, sometimes unique knowledge, sometimes all three.

The trick is to create an environment in which this uniqueness emerges quickly but naturally and not leave it to be discovered at the end of the project or worse still in the leaving speeches. Things aren't helped by the fact that people often don't realise their special talents until they are pointed out to them. It may mean doing a bit of experimentation and taking the odd risk just to understand what their capabilities are.

What's great is that once someone's unique value is understood by everybody, morale improves immediately. For the individual it instantly creates self-esteem and a reason for being around. For the team it means that it can be confident that its collective competence is being fully leveraged.

Many years ago I worked with a computer operator who it seemed was only capable of mounting magnetic tapes. When he retired we discovered that outside work he was a top notch ice-dancing coach and had won numerous awards. Surely some of that ability could have been put to use during working hours.

Short ropes v. long ropes

It's a Monday morning and eyeballing you from across the table is the newest recruit to your team. You're about to describe her first assignment and can't decide how much guidance to give. The c.v. and interview were good but this is high profile stuff and mistakes will rebound on you.

The big question – do you give her a short or a long rope? This is an exceedingly important issue which if ducked or answered wrongly could give a lot of grief in the months to come.

Short rope proponents are risk averse and start out giving very little freedom with the intention down the line to let the rope out little by little "when she is ready". The problem with this is that out of frustration she may take her ball home and leave and you'll never find out what she's really capable of.

Long rope proponents would give her a great deal of initial latitude to identify her strengths early on and stand on the touch line ready to catch the stray ball. Where weaknesses emerge the box of tissues is ready and the rope is rapidly pulled in. This approach is harder to manage as people are often too proud to own up when they are in difficulty. It can also permanently damage their emerging reputation if things go wrong.

Best of all is to have not one but several ropes, some long and some short. Keep a tight rein where absolutely necessary but make it clear why you're doing so. Where it's not necessary make it equally clear why you're taking the risk and what you're expecting. That way you'll both be happy.

Managing meetings

How many hours per day do you waste in badly run meetings? How much frustration do you feel when yet again you've sat helpless participating in one of the main causes of lost management time?

We've all seen what happens when either no one takes the chair or, worse still, someone tries to but fails. The meeting has no clear objective. The attendees are not sure why they are there. No one has done any preparation. The discussion rambles on with no clear conclusion. No actions are recorded. No follow up takes place.

It's worth asking why otherwise intelligent people allow this to happen. Sometimes it suits participants to have chaos. That way unwelcome decisions are not made. Usually I suspect it's because we stick to the naïve belief that individually intelligent people will automatically form a group that behaves intelligently when gathered together.

There is no substitute for having a well prepared chairman who makes sure everyone knows what the meeting's for (communication, discussion, decisions, etc.), knows why everyone's there, keeps the discussion on track, encourages the hesitant, sits on the verbose, keeps to time, brings things to conclusion and agrees next steps.

Next time you find yourself in a badly run meeting do a quick estimate of the combined salary bill for all the participants and then calculate the cost to the enterprise of each wasted 'meeting hour'. That will demonstrate the value of good meeting management.

Saying well done

A defining characteristic of good people managers is their ability to say "well done!" both frequently and with feeling. Nothing can more quickly improve the motivation and performance of an individual than a deserved pat on the back.

It is so easy to do but, as a standard management technique, frequently forgotten or ignored. Parents shower praise on their children for the smallest of achievements – the first step, the first word, the first good school report – and delight in the glow on the face that results. These same parents, when at work, often throw all this learning away and for some inexplicable reason assume their staff, being mature adults, are somehow 'beyond' this and don't need encouragement.

Why do they do this? Perhaps it's felt to be 'un-British' for the giver and receiver to indulge in such wimpish behaviour.

Perhaps it's because the manager doesn't think that praise is important because he never had any, so why should his staff? "Let them learn the hard way."

Perhaps it's because giving praise is seen as a sign of weakness, letting the guard down and hence threatening future authority. In fact the contrary is usually the case. Witness military practice where reward and authority go hand in hand.

So take courage. Don't be afraid. Go out there and congratulate people for work well done. You'll be amazed at the results.

Thinkers and doers

I know I'm being extremely simplistic but I've always found it useful to categorise people as either thinkers or as doers. The thinkers are never happier than when presented with a new intellectual challenge and a 'blank sheet of paper'. The doers on the other hand like to deliver things and fast – "let's cut out the talk and get on with it".

Whatever the task you'll always need a mixture of thinkers and doers, only the proportions will vary. Your responsibility as manager is to keep both groups motivated and singing from the same hymn sheet. This is hard for several reasons:

- The relative importance of each skill tends to vary over the lifetime of an assignment. Thinking skills are needed early on when ideas are being formed. Doing skills are critical later when things have to be delivered.

- What motivates each group is different, and therefore trying to create a common purpose can be very difficult.

- There may not be much mutual respect, so as manager you'll have to do a lot of 'translating' and arbitrating.

Good people managers recognise these issues early on, and find ways to 'build bridges' between the groups. If Alice and Bill are the brains and Chris and Donna are the deliverers why not pair up Alice and Chris on some small task. Doers like the support of thinkers (in small doses) and vice versa. The most powerful solution, however, is the simplest – just take the time to recognise publicly the contribution of both your thinkers and your doers.

Falling down holes

"If you don't let people fall down small holes, they won't spot the large hole when it arrives".

People learn by mistakes. The jarring effect of making a major bloomer often leaves a powerful memory for years afterwards and a desperate desire never to be in the same position again. "If only I'd been at that meeting on time." "If only I'd got the figures right at that presentation." "If only I'd kept my mouth shut and hadn't embarrassed my boss in front of his peers."

One of the biggest misjudgements made by otherwise competent managers is to protect their staff from making blunders. This is rarely done for altruistic reasons. Sometimes it's done to keep things moving. Sometimes it's done to avoid unnecessary costs. Often it's because the manager doesn't like grovelling to others, particularly when the mistake could have been avoided.

So what happens? The boss is away, or a new boss arrives, and a crisis (the big hole) hits. It's mishandled through lack of experience and everyone shouts "What's the matter with these guys? Where have they been all this time? Haven't they learned anything?"

Motto – give your people space. Don't mollycoddle them. Encourage risk-taking. Let them learn through their mistakes. Practise apologising.

Personal contracts

There was a time when money was a sufficient motivator – a fair day's work for a fair day's pay.

There was then a time when the motivation came from achieving things, often as part of a team, in the hope that the eventual glory would be shared and the subsequent career would benefit.

We now are in a world where people expect, quite legitimately, that in return for their helping to grow the enterprise, the enterprise will help grow them as individuals and will commit to such growth. In crude terms, if the venture I'm involved with goes belly up at least I'll have got something out of it.

This is where the idea of a 'personal contract' comes in. When agreeing to a job my personal contract is signed both by myself and by my boss.

In part A I sign up to the usual accountabilities and end of year performance objectives.

In part B my boss signs up to a list of the things I want out of the job – exposure to key stakeholders, development of new skills, sufficient headroom, etc. – provided these can be made compatible with part A.

Part B requires hard thinking. It also requires argument and compromise but, if fully bought into by both parties, can be a great platform on which to build a long lasting relationship.

Everyone's a coach

Those of us who've frequently moved jobs will have a file of farewell notes from ex colleagues. In mine, my favourite includes the following: "Thanks for all your help. I learned a lot from you". For me, and I guess for many of you, the realisation that you've passed on some of your knowledge and that it is appreciated creates a very warm feeling.

I find it curious that we think of coaching as something to be provided by experts rather than as a basic requirement of the job. As managers, we may not be interested in developing our people. We may believe that we'd be hopeless at it, but, whether we like it or not, our people look to us for advice and will pick up our knowledge however difficult we make it for them.

At the end of the day, whatever the text books say the basics of coaching aren't that hard. As a minimum it requires:

- time to talk with your 'coachee' not about the job but about how he/she can develop while doing the job. I don't go with the annual 'appraisal' – much better to do this as and when necessary.

- focus on the areas needing development and a mutual agreement on how this can best be achieved including taking on new responsibilities 'as a trial'.

- patience on your part when things don't go well and your colleague needs sympathy and encouragement. Developing people can be a long haul but the pay-offs are enormous.

All of us would like to be remembered after we're gone. To be willing and able to pass on something of yourself to those who work for you must be one of the most rewarding ways of achieving immortality.

Extraordinary performance

I can still remember, over 30 years later, my first boss taking me on one side one day, and describing a particular individual in our team saying "XXXX is not just 10% better at what he does than anyone else, he's 100% better".

We carry around the view that wide variations around the mean are the exceptions rather than the rule. In my experience this does not apply to people's performance. Given the right guidance and environment individuals and teams can produce quite astonishing results, way beyond anyone's expectations. There's frequently no logic to it and it can be totally unexpected when it occurs.

In the case of individuals it's often to do with finding the square hole into which the square peg will fit. For years I remember struggling with a computer programmer who just wouldn't cut it no matter how hard we both tried. Then almost by accident we discovered that he had both a penchant and an aptitude for staff training and from that moment his career took off.

In the case of teams, it's something to do with personal chemistry supported by a clear goal and the sprinkling of 'magic dust' by a good leader. When teams go into overdrive everyone around can sense it – the atmosphere's electric, the faces are alight and there's an amazing ability to get things done almost without effort. I don't know of any way to force a team to outperform – you just have to thank your lucky stars when it happens.

The lesson I think from all this is always to be optimistic rather than pessimistic about what your people can achieve. By creating the conditions for extraordinary performance you may wake up one day and get a big surprise.

Co-operative career planning

Uncertainty is everywhere. Organisations have to face up to it every day and develop appropriate coping strategies. One area of uncertainty, however, that is often not well handled relates to the way individuals and organisations interact, the vexing problem of career planning.

It's the classic conundrum. The individual wants to know as much as possible about where he/she is going next year and in future years so that some sort of 'life plan' can be made. The organisation wants to make as few promises as possible to avoid giving commitments that for one reason or another can't be met. The result is often that, through the absence of any established good practice, neither party is happy – good people leave and less good people get promoted.

I have long argued that a compromise is possible provided there's give and take on either side. What's wrong with creating a 'skeletal' career plan for each individual, saying what they might expect to happen given a following wind?

What would such a plan look like?

1.   It would cover a long time period – at least 5 to 10 years.

2.   It would be 'broad brush' and talk about job levels rather than specific jobs.

3.   It would define an individual's likely ceiling (where there is one).

4.   It would set out the underlying assumptions – available slots, development needs, etc.

5.   It would not make any firm promises.

Some would argue that such a career plan could be demotivational as it contains no guarantees. I would argue quite the opposite – people need something to strive for and are usually big enough to cope with the possible disappointment if they don't succeed.

Part 3

People Influencing

Sitting on the opposite side of the table as you speak

Influencing others and winning them round is now one of life's essentials in any organisation. It's hard when they're more senior than you. It's harder when you don't report to them. It's harder still when they don't want to listen, for example if you're advocating an uncomfortable course of action or giving bad news (the whistleblower's problem).

When planning such an encounter the temptation is to think solely about the arguments and the words, i.e. the content of the dialogue. Research has shown, however, that success comes as much from how you conduct yourself as from what you say.

For the influencer there are two great skills that should be cultivated. The first is learning to observe yourself, if possible, while actually engaged in influencing. How do I sound? Am I sounding coherent? Am I sounding nervous? Am I using the right language?

The second skill is learning to observe, to really observe the subject of your influence. Is she listening? Are her eyes wandering? Is she dying to get in a word? Is she shuffling in her seat?

If you learn the art of 'sitting on the other side of the table as you speak' it will be much easier to judge the success of your influencing and decide whether to persist or to cut and run (sometimes the best strategy). That way much heartache can be avoided.

Explaining through examples

A most underutilised tool in the influencer's kitbag is the use of examples. We all delight in putting together cogent arguments filled with a compelling rationale, succinct recommendations and unarguable next steps. Yet in spite of all this, sometimes people still don't get it.

Perhaps we should descend from our lofty pedestal and use the time-honoured technique of 'parable' (as used by Christ) or 'discourse' (as used by the Buddha). These, two of the world's greatest ever influencers, found that it was only by example that difficult messages could be hammered home and hearts and minds won over.

Many people aren't conceptual thinkers, even if they believe and say they are. For them a single striking example can bring a subject alive and suddenly the clouds will clear and the point will be understood.

Several years ago I found myself trying to explain to manufacturing workers the concept of 'portfolio management' – the idea that most consumer products can be derived from a small 'portfolio' of standard components but assembled in a unique fashion. Try as we might the message didn't hit home until my colleague suddenly announced "Did you know that today we use 19 different thicknesses of cardboard in our toothpaste cartons!" Nothing more had to be said.

The wonder of humour

Why do we take ourselves so seriously all the time? It's not just ourselves as individuals; it's the organisations we work for, the 'brand name' we support, the mission statement we follow. Sorry to be irreverent, but I must ask the question since a consequence of all this seriousness is that humour often gets pushed to the back burner. We thus lose not only a great escape valve but also, most importantly, one of the best means I know of breaking down barriers.

You know the situation. You've been summoned to the board meeting to explain your proposal and find yourself surrounded by a lot of smart suits all exuding seriousness and gravitas. There is now a choice: either maintain the solemnity and probably fail to get any effective dialogue, or find a way to lighten the mood. At the very least indulge in some self-inflicted leg-pulling.

It's the same with large gatherings. I've seen these drag on amidst increasing signs of tension and frustration until someone had the sense to show a silly picture, or tell a funny story and suddenly it was as if a heavy fog had lifted and lightness descended on the gathering.

The great thing about using humour is that all those things that divide people – status, background, knowledge, accent, etc. – disappear instantly when a dose of humour is applied.

Several years ago at the start of a senior management conference I introduced without warning a short clip of Billy Connolly talking colourfully about the "bottom line". There was a moment of horror on the CEO's face then he suddenly burst into hysterical laughter and everyone else followed – the ice was broken and the proceedings thereafter were a stunning success.

Different mental models

One of the biggest difficulties facing people who need to influence others is coping with the fact that different people think differently and have different mental models.

Some of us, the 'engineers', think from the inside outwards. We picture everything as a machine or set of processes. Changing things is just about recognising how processes need to change and doing it.

Some of us, the 'marketeers', think from the outside inwards. We try at all times to sit in the customers' shoes and imagine how they will feel about what is proposed. If the activity has no customer impact it is at best irrelevant.

Some of us, the 'motivators', see everything through people whether they be employees, customers, shareholders or society. For us the key thing is how people will react to what is proposed.

As the influencer, what do you do when faced with this? The first thing is to work out what type of animal you're dealing with – this can only come from hard listening.

After that, it's about adapting the way you speak, the language you use, the things you focus on, and continuing to listen hard. I describe it as the 'chameleon' approach to dealing with people. It may feel like you're compromising your position but some sensitivity in this area can pay huge dividends.

Empathy – the magic ingredient for communicators

What makes the difference between a good communicator and a great communicator? One word: empathy – the ability to relate to your audience and get them on side.

A good communicator knows what he wants to say, talks clearly and concisely, even throws in some humour but can still leave an audience cold. A great communicator holds the audience in the palm of his hand by finding ways to bring his audience close to what he is feeling and thinking.

It's not easy as it's a lot to do with personality – warmth and intuition play a large part. But there are various techniques which if used carefully can help increase the bond with your listeners.

With an audience you know well, the simplest is to bring people into the story – "as I said to Joe the other day…" Instantly Joe and his mates are on side, even if he's forgotten what you said.

More subtle is to describe personal situations, often humorous, which members of the audience may have experienced themselves and to which they can relate. A bit of self-deprecation can work wonders.

More direct is to conduct live dialogues, questions and answers, to get people involved – the teacher's trick. This is the most dangerous but it can be very effective for getting collective ownership of an issue.

Whatever technique you use, the aim is the same: to form a relationship with your audience and start to win them over.

Why before what before how before who

When you're in the business of influencing people which most of us are most of the time it helps to have a few rules of thumb. Of these one of the most useful I've found is to remind myself every time:

- what I'm proposing should be done

- why I'm proposing it

- how I'm expecting to organise things including timescales

- who I think will be affected in one way or another.

It's obvious isn't it, so obvious that those who are doing the influencing often forget one of the four pieces. They assume people understand and agree the rationale for action, the 'why' – a very dangerous assumption even for things that have been discussed for ages.

They assume that everyone realises what's involved, the 'how'. If you're batting in foreign territory, for example describing systems implementation to non systems people, don't for heavens sake make any assumptions here – quite the reverse, overkill is often necessary.

Worst of all, influencers often underplay the effect on people of what's being proposed – the 'who'. Here we're talking about those affected both directly and indirectly, and what they'll be expected to contribute.

By organising your thinking this way you'll also find it easier to tailor what you're saying to different audiences with different interests, often one of the biggest challenges.

Readers and listeners

Most people can be categorised as being either good readers or good listeners but not both.

Readers are most comfortable absorbing written information at their own speed in their own company and without the distraction of someone sounding off in an incomprehensible illogical fashion.

Listeners on the other hand believe that words constitute only a small part of the whole story and rely much more on tone of voice, implied rather than spoken meaning and, most importantly, on the opportunity to probe and ask questions.

When, as leader, change agent or consultant, your job is to influence people, it is really helpful to know whether the subject of your influence is a reader or a listener. I have seen huge amounts of time wasted on beautifully crafted reports when some well-chosen words would have been sufficient. Equally the experience of painstakingly trying to explain something which ultimately 'falls on deaf ears' can be most depressing.

The real challenge comes when you have to influence a mixed group of readers and listeners. When this happens there is no alternative but to provide both a spoken presentation and a separate written report. For goodness sake don't fall into the common trap of trying to do both together – our eyes aren't designed to take in crowded PowerPoint screens!

* with acknowledgement to Peter Drucker, 'Managing Yourself', *Harvard Business Review*, Mar/Apr 1999

Getting those messages across

I can still remember the occasion. It was early in my career. I was asked to explain our various computer systems to some visiting bigwig and spent ages constructing a beautiful diagram which I thought a masterpiece of clarity only to have it thrown back in my face and asked to write some simple text instead. The lesson I learned is that when you're trying to get a message across what seems clear to you may be far from clear to others.

We all have our favourite approaches when trying to influence others. Some of us are happiest with the written word and enjoy devising finely honed sentences. Some of us like drawing sketches and keep a huge heap of scrap paper at the ready. Some of us prefer simply to talk and we paint pictures as we speak using analogies and stories.

The problem in organisations is how to enable large numbers of people to get large numbers of messages across both efficiently and effectively. My reluctant conclusion after numerous head-bashings is that nothing beats having a 'house style' – a standard way of laying out documents for everyone to follow whatever the type of message being communicated. If well designed, the standard should encompass the whole range of documents with which one has to deal from formal proposals to informal discussion papers.

On the surface this might seem an unnecessary constraint on creativity. In practice what I've found is that busy executives bombarded with paper need a house style as a comfort blanket to help them get through their days.

When the chips are down you're much more likely to get your message across to a comfortable executive than an uncomfortable one.

Tying your flag to multiple poles

All of us at some stage in our working lives have to decide whether we wish to get to the top of our chosen profession, and if so, how best to get there. Part of the 'how' is in fact a question of 'who', i.e. who from among the senior management can and will help us in our rise to the top and hence provide a 'pole' to which we can tie our 'flag'.

Some people take this very seriously and work assiduously on developing sponsors. Others, the less political, leave things more to chance and hope that someone 'up there' is looking after their interests. The big question in either case is whether to rely on a single individual or to cultivate a number of senior supporters.

The former option can be brilliant while he or she is in the ascendant, but it's obviously a high risk strategy. We have all seen the failure of one individual bringing down others in the resulting wake.

The latter option is much harder work. It means keeping in with everybody and learning to adapt easily to people's different mental models and ways of doing things. It also means occasionally having to play the role of 'message carrier' when there are high-level disagreements.

As a general rule, if it's quick advancement you're looking for then find the highest flier and stick to him or her. If you're interested in long-term survival, spread your bets and tie your flag to multiple poles.

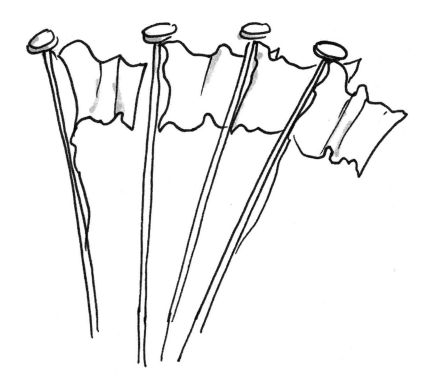

The sad story of the internal consultant

It always starts so well. You get a summons to the MD's office. "We've got a special project for you and one for which you're ideally suited. Here's the brief (a half side of A4 if you're lucky). We expect it to take around 4 months. Good luck". You leave on cloud nine believing that the career has taken a big leap forward and greater things are in store.

What's actually happening is that the top brass have an issue that they can't or won't resolve. To save face they commission a study in order to be seen to be doing something and then look for the nearest available manager who happens to be free.

This is the world of the internal consultant, a breed of people who deserve our sympathy because they do the jobs no one else wants because the work is either too difficult, too political or simply going nowhere.

So how does one succeed in such circumstances? A few starting tips:

1. Take time agreeing a scope and objectives that are actually achievable.

2. Find at least one top level sponsor who's interested in the outcome and prepared to spend time giving advice and support.

3. Build up a network of competent and credible people to act as 'sounding boards'.

4. Stay out of the politics and don't go for personal Brownie points.

The key thing to keep in mind is that internal consultants (unlike their external counterparts) come 'free' – there is a high risk therefore that unpalatable messages may simply be ignored. Unfortunately, as the Americans so aptly put it, this is the way the cookie often crumbles.

Part 4

Teams

Teams are everywhere

I am continually surprised that people talk about teams and team working as if they were somehow an option that you can take or leave. I find it hard to think of any endeavour anywhere that can be successful these days without an effective team behind it. Even the solo round-the-world yachtswoman needs a team – in her case as the essential support mechanism.

So what lies behind the view that teams are optional? Perhaps it's because setting up effective teams takes lots of time and effort. Perhaps it's because strong teams threaten the power of individuals who need to feel that they are in charge and hold personal accountability.

Whatever the reason I would argue that today's problems are so complex that having a group of people with a mixture of skills interacting with each other is usually the best and the quickest approach to solving them. This may require a permanent team (i.e. fixed in the organisation structure), a temporary working party or a cross-functional network.

The crucial point, though, is that leaders of such teams and such organisations have to behave not as heads of a cavalry charge but as conductors of an orchestra. Their key responsibility is to 'create the space' to get the best from their people. They are still accountable for the decisions and the organisation's outputs but the results are achieved in a very different way.

Team fundamentals

Whatever the task at hand from a multi-year project to a short study it almost always involves a team – a group of people who collectively have the competence to perform what is required.

Successful teams do not, however, emerge automatically from putting together people with the right skills, even when everyone is highly motivated and keen to get started. For all the talk about the importance of team-building, it is astonishing how often this simple fact is forgotten. Creating powerful teams takes effort, perseverance and lots of time.

Three fundamentals are needed for teams to be successful:

1. A clear goal to which everyone is both intellectually and emotionally committed. The intellectual support is needed from day one – the emotional may take longer.

2. Clear individual accountabilities so that everyone knows at all times what is expected of them. Again, it may take a few weeks for precise accountabilities to be honed down.

3. A leader who maintains the clarity of the goal, manages the accountabilities and creates a supportive environment with mutual respect and trust.

Time is needed to explain the goal and secure people's emotional commitment. More time is needed to agree accountabilities. Even more time is needed to build up a good team atmosphere. But the eventual prizes, if you invest the time at the start, will be enormous.

Leading teams

You may have done it dozens of times but taking on the leadership of a new team is never easy. On day one there you are at the head of the table surrounded by a group of expectant faces all eager to take up the new challenge. Quietly you're thinking to yourself: Is this project do-able? Have these people got the right skills? Will they get on together? How long will it take to make them really effective?

For me the nearest equivalent is that of an orchestral conductor who has both to ensure that everyone follows his beat and at the same time to give individual players sufficient latitude to show off their talents. The best conductors get this balance just right.

So it is with team leaders, the greatest of whom are both demanding and inspirational – demanding in terms of the goals to be achieved and the rules to be followed, inspirational in their ability to draw out the very best from their colleagues and get them to 'go the extra mile' without using the whip.

To be demanding and inspirational at the same time isn't easy. It requires both confidence and humility, the latter from a recognition that whatever is ultimately achieved will be 99% the work of the team members, not yourself. They are the stars. They are the heroes. They deserve the applause when things go well. As team leader you are merely the lighter that sets off the fireworks.

Collective responsibility

As a team leader you know you've made it when one day you're ill, a major crisis takes place, nobody phones and you come in the next day to find order restored and no serious repercussions taking place. The first emotion on returning is often a disappointment that your unique skills weren't needed. A better emotion is that of pride that you've created a team capable of assuming collective responsibility when it counts.

Once you've achieved it, the power of such a team is tremendous. Suddenly things happen without discussion. The weekly team meetings get shorter and more focused. The endless worrying about whether Joan and Bill will ever get on seems somehow irrelevant. Most importantly your role as team leader moves up a notch from hands-on manager to leader and coach, from concern about today to planning for tomorrow.

You may not want such a team. You may fear losing personal power. If on the other hand you do, then I would suggest that some hard thinking is needed about how to bring it about.

Start by thinking how you spend your time and consider delegating more. Then watch and listen to the team's behaviour. Do they understand each other's roles and what they bring to the party? Do they respect and trust each other? If not is there a 'bad apple' that needs to be removed? Are they all emotionally committed to pulling this off?

It's not rocket science. It can be done, but as team leader you have to want it to happen and be prepared to put in serious effort to make it happen. Then you can pamper yourself and make the most of those days off.

Great teams

Most over-40s can tell you a story about "the best job they ever had" which was both a lot of fun and hugely successful. Almost invariably after probing you'll find that at its heart was a great team of people – not just a good team but a great team.

The question is, why aren't all teams great teams? What stops a competent manager, given a group of people as his raw material, from welding it together to make an exceptional working unit?

From my experience, several things get in the way. The first and most obvious is a fear of losing control. "If my team starts to take off, how can I keep it pointing in the right direction? How will I cope when the boss comes round asking questions? How will I fill my day?" In other words, a fear of the unknown.

The second inhibitor is not knowing how to go about team-building. Holding an initial workshop is a good start and there are lots of skilled facilitators. The clever thing, though, is to find ways to reinforce this continually, if possible on a daily basis.

The final barrier, and probably the most important, is that many managers deep down don't really understand the amazing power of a great team. It's the buzz and excitement of a group of people who act as foils for each other, who each know their role and by working together are able to achieve much more than the sum of the parts.

Whatever is stopping you, let me let me urge you to cast aside your inhibitions and have a go. Take a chance. Trust your judgement. Let your people show you what they can accomplish as a great team.

Part 5

Organisation Change

Don't reach for the organisation chart

On day one of a new job what is the first thing you want to know? Probably who the key players are, how things get done around there, and what you should watch out for. And what are you presented with? A chart showing the organisation's reporting structure.

It is worth asking whether a simple picture with boxes and lines really describes how an organisation works. People do need to know who's responsible for pay and rations and who does their annual appraisal but that's about the limit of the chart's usefulness.

If you are really trying to understand how things work then you have to turn to what's not written down rather than what is.

Start by asking what are the assumptions underpinning actions and decisions. There will be assumptions about the external environment such as competitors, the organisation's core capabilities and, most importantly, what's acceptable in terms of behaviour.

Go on to ask about the main management processes – how are decisions made, what are the key meetings, what is the annual planning calendar, what are the most important data sources, etc.

Finally, try to find out (and this will be difficult) something about the informal networks that operate around the place – who's close to whom, who do the top brass use as sounding boards, which are the main warring factions.

Assemble these 'unwritten rules' and you will understand how the organisation actually works and, if asked, how to change it.

The five dimensions of organisational change

Try looking on Amazon for books on 'organisational change' – I have and I've found hundreds. Why? Because all the consultants and gurus have their own theories and models concerning what is, after all, the biggest challenge faced by any enterprise.

If you sift through it I would argue that there are five things, and only five, that you need to think about when changing an organisation. They divide into two groups: three 'hard' – process, structure and systems – and two 'soft' – competencies and behaviours.

The hard dimensions are all about how the work is done – the processes that people at all levels have to follow, who is responsible for what (the structure), and what part IT plays in it all. I describe these as 'hard' since much can be written down and there are rules about how best to design and implement such changes.

In contrast the soft dimensions, being about people, are much more difficult to define and therefore much tougher to change. Certainly, you can write down the skills people need but education and training are never easy. And as for behaviours, the 'will' rather than the 'skill', whole books have been written about how to approach behavioural change, so complex an issue is it.

The lesson I've learnt over the years is that whatever anyone tells you, you'll almost always need to think about every one of the five dimensions and you should worry if one or more is missing – this is probably a major oversight.

Emotional commitment (1)

The words 'emotional commitment' don't often get a mention around management tables where it is often assumed that if a course of action is based on logic everything else will follow. At times of organisational change this can be disastrous – failure to acquire and retain the emotional commitment of people affected is one of the main reasons change programmes fail.

Picture the scene – a big presentation from the top brass. "We need to change the way we do things around here. We all need to change. The success of the business demands it!" Everyone nods their heads. Intellectually it all makes sense that is unarguable. But deep down it feels as if this has been imposed from on high and hasn't come from thinking about the needs or desires of each individual.

So what happens? The programme goes ahead. The resources are mobilised. The systems are developed. The people are trained. There's a big implementation, and then things start going wrong, little things at first but then more and more issues emerge from the woodwork. The top brass don't understand what's going on – wasn't everyone consulted when all this was designed?

Organisation change is so intrinsically difficult that it needs the knowledge, creativity and drive of the people directly affected if it is to achieve its objectives. These won't materialise without their emotional commitment.

How to get emotional commitment is another story ….

The power of planning

We've all heard the stories. "Yet one more large IT project goes off the rails. Three years late and £200 million over budget!" It's not just IT; it happens all over the place. If you dig deep, I suspect that you'll find that once again poor planning was a major contributory factor.

But what is good planning? Everyone knows that you need a plan, that's obvious. What's less well known is that, if done well, planning can be an incredibly powerful management mechanism which acts as the 'glue' to hold everything and everyone together.

To be really good, planning must satisfy several criteria:

- It must be dynamic. Plans which don't change to reflect what's achievable on the ground are a waste of time. A 'macho' approach which ignores reality always comes to grief in the long term.

- It must be multi-layered and hence separable into relatively independent but connected pieces. Constructing such sub plans is often the toughest part of starting a project.

- It must be enforced. This means that the plans must be easily understood, well communicated and totally embedded in the overall management process. Every project manager should insist on having a first rate planner as a key support.

In 1944 the world witnessed one of the most extraordinary projects in the history of warfare, landing a million men on the beaches of Normandy. Just reflect for a moment on the quality of planning that went into that.

Would you start from here?

A common problem when designing organisation changes is trying to get people to think outside the box. Everyone, particularly the long servers, comes with a long list of assumptions of "how things are around here" which act as a smoky lens through which they view any proposal for change. It's not their fault; it's a law of nature.

A good question to get things moving is to ask "If you could start all over again with a blank sheet of paper, what would things be like around here?" Suddenly the floodgates open and all those pent-up ideas long suppressed come flooding out.

The focus moves to considering what the organisation is really about and how it actually needs to operate at the coalface:

"Why does that document have to be checked by so many people?" "Why do we run this ourselves? Surely it would be done better by an external agency?" "Why can't that decision be made by one person not ten?" "With a decent system couldn't we do this in days rather than months?" – and so on.

The great thing is that people begin to break out of their old way of thinking and start acting as co-creators of a new world. It also becomes fun!

My favourite example of not starting from here must be the daily trauma faced by service suppliers of water, gas, electricity, etc., forced to disrupt transport in order to make changes and fix problems. If we were starting again, surely the pipes and cables would go alongside roads not under them.

Half-way pendulums

How often have you heard someone say "We tried this before. It didn't work then, so why should it work now?" This is often the result of the swinging pendulum effect – moving from one extreme to the other without considering whether stopping half way wouldn't be a better approach.

You see it everywhere. First we centralise, then we decentralise. First it's command and control, then it's unlimited empowerment. First it's individual accountability, then it's team working. First it's smart casual, then it's business dress. And so on.

The problem is that to get people to change, we believe that the message has to be oversold if anyone is to take notice. "We need a radically different vision for this business if people are to follow us!"

Often quite the reverse is the case. People and organisations get change fatigue. What they want are leaders who can see all points of view and choose the best bits of each. Why centralise or decentralise? Why not centralise some bits and decentralise others? Why choose between control and empowerment? Why not provide a control framework in which people are empowered?

It's time to treat people as adults who will understand, provided you take the time to explain, that a half-way pendulum may well be the wisest course.

Sequencing organisation change

One of the most important decisions when planning large-scale organisation change is the sequence in which to do things. In my experience an organisation's capacity for change is finite – often constrained by the pressures of the day-to-day business, the funds available and the experience of senior managers. With a large list of things to be done, getting agreement on what should be done when is critical.

Some things are obvious. A stand-alone initiative with fast payback may well, apart from the financial benefit, serve as an excellent 'marketing' tool to help sell a change programme. Equally obvious is the need to move fast when you're starting multi-year systems changes as these invariably take longer than planned.

For the rest I have found the following questions helpful:

- What is most in tune with current business focus and hence likely to get most support from business leaders?

- What appears to carry most risk? Would the risk be reduced if we waited for more information?

- Are there some foundation pieces that will make everything else easier? I describe these as the 'bottom layer of bricks'. Personnel changes, such as the removal of obstructing managers, often fall into this category.

Don't duck these questions and try to do everything immediately – therein lies mayhem. Agree a sequence and then the detailed planning can begin.

Pity the project manager

I call them the unsung heroes of our time. They do the nasty jobs that sensible people wouldn't touch with a bargepole because they're too high risk and often career-limiting. I'm talking, of course, about project managers who you'll find struggling against the odds in most parts of today's organisations.

The irony is that much of what project managers do is within the scope of any manager. Our lives are full of projects – buying a house, preparing for a dinner party, going on holiday, planning the daughter's wedding – all of these require planning and coordination and all of us (or nearly all of us) seem able to pull them off without fuss.

So it's worth asking why when we're at work we so often dump everything on the poor project manager and let him or her do all the worrying.

Contrary to popular belief I suggest that it's much more about will than skill. We choose to let project managers worry about everything – maintaining the forward plan, checking that the funds and people are available, checking that the work's been done properly and on time, checking that all the different stakeholders are happy – in other words carrying the can for everything.

A much better and safer way to operate is to recognise that everyone has both a responsibility for the success of key projects and also the ability to get involved. Perhaps once in a while we should show some sympathy and give the project manager a break.

Emotional commitment (2)

OK, so you've read the textbook and understand that you have to work on the hearts and minds of the people on whom you're foisting this new performance management process. The first big presentation is tomorrow – 100 product buyers all wondering why they've been dragged from their work when there's money to be made. So how do you go about it?

Well on this occasion let me suggest some 'don'ts' rather than 'do's':

Rule 1   Don't sugar the pill. If there are hard messages about what's driving the changes or about its implications don't try to cover them up – people aren't stupid.

Rule 2   Don't underplay the benefits. If you have high ambitions for what can be achieved, then it's your job to 'sell' these to the recipients.

Rule 3   Don't pretend you know all the answers. One of the quickest ways to get people engaged is to seek their help in designing whatever changes are necessary

Rule 4   Don't cover up uncertainties but do tell people everything you can. Also tell them when you hope to be more certain.

Rule 5   Don't ever conceal the truth. Changing things is all about trust – tell them porkies and they'll never trust you.

Finally one 'do' – do be yourself. Winning people over is one of the hardest jobs there is. Ultimately it's about transferring your enthusiasm to your audience – only you know how best to do that.

Communicating by drumbeat

Ask any consumer product manufacturer about building brands. Ask any daily cartoonist about creating political caricatures. Ask any media guru about grooming film stars. The message from all three will be about endless repetition of the same story week in week out.

When you're changing an organisation for whatever reason the same lesson applies. You have to be prepared to invest large amounts of time explaining over and over again the key messages – what's going to be happening, why we're doing it, how and when it will be implemented and who will be affected. I call it communicating by 'drumbeat'.

It's not that people are stupid or unwilling to listen. It's not even that they're too preoccupied with other things. It's more because changing the way things operate – the responsibilities, the activities or the systems – is very difficult stuff, which takes a lot of understanding. It's also – and this is really important – about both the head and the heart.

I talk elsewhere about emotional commitment. While a good kick-off for any change programme is essential, the winning over of hearts as well as minds takes time – lots of time. People may get the intellectual story quickly; they will only absorb the personal implications over time and with the help of an endlessly repeating drumbeat.

Changing at the right pace

Probably the biggest challenge faced by those responsible for leading organisation change is choosing the right pace. When you're changing structures, processes or systems the end point may be clear. What is often not clear is the best way to get there and the optimal time over which to make it all happen.

I've found that there is usually no simple answer. "As fast as possible" is often the worst possible choice although, if the situation is serious enough, this might seem unavoidable.

Several things need to be considered:

- What else is happening in the enterprise (and hence how much management attention will this get)?

- How much experience is there of this kind of change and hence how much time will be needed for making mistakes?

- How long can the motivation of the change agents be maintained?

- Can we break things into little chunks each of which can be implemented fast?

For some things, like the installation of new systems, there is often a case for starting with a long slow pilot and then speeding up rapidly once you're confident that everything works. For other things, such as trying to change the culture, a big shock (e.g. mass redundancy) may be needed at the start followed by a multi-year consolidation.

The key point is to recognise that time talking about the pace of change is time well spent.

Forget values, concentrate on behaviours

Call me old-fashioned if you like, but some consulting techniques get right up my nose – in particular, the endless desire to explore the motivations behind the way people behave.

Picture the scene. A young facilitator leading a session on the company's mission and values asks Mrs Stephens what her personal 'values' are. With a demanding spouse, demanding children and a demanding house to run, how much time do you think she spends contemplating what makes her tick? And what business is it anyway of anyone else?

Such discussions are driven by a belief that if you understand people's motivations you can explain their behaviours and thereby be in a position to alter them – often a critical requirement when orchestrating large scale organisation change.

Why do we dance in this way around the behaviour question? Time and time again I've seen managers shirking the simple job of telling people what behaviours are expected, what will not be acceptable, and what will happen if you break these 'rules'. If the rule is that teamwork is in and mutual support is to be the norm then for goodness sake tell people in no uncertain terms how you'll react to solo operators who pursue their own agenda.

Many years ago I found myself chairing a workshop concerned with changing product development processes. I thought we'd covered everything until a junior voice from the floor said "Haven't you forgotten something? Unless we change the way people behave this will all be a waste of time." The moral: don't dance around behaviours – confront them head on. That's what troops expect from their leaders.

Managing uncertainty

A constant dilemma faced by leaders of organisation change is how to manage uncertainty – or specifically, how to manage the people facing uncertainty.

By its very nature, organisation change is usually too complex to enable every aspect of the change journey to be mapped out in advance. This is particularly true when the elapsed time runs into years. The general direction 'north not south' is normally clear – the fact that it ends up as NNE may take some time to emerge.

People however like to know what's in store for them. Is their job safe? Will they have to retrain? Will they be getting a new boss? When will everything happen?

I've found that the best, indeed the only, way to handle this is by committing to maximum openness and a process of 'managed news releases'. At each stage it means saying "this is all I can tell you now – I'll have more information on X on dd/mm/yy". Provided that both statements are true people will begin to stop worrying.

Making such commitments of course creates its own discipline for those leading the changes – it forces timely decision-making and puts good planning at a premium. The benefit though in terms of people commitment can be enormous. If done consistently it will lead to genuine trust – the biggest prize in a time of uncertainty.

Transferring ownership

My apologies for using a hackneyed phrase but the issue of 'ownership' when you're in the midst of organisation change remains one of the thorniest problems you're likely to face.

What are we talking about here? Typical scenario – a departmental manager is told that new systems are coming in and that headcount savings of 30% will be expected as a result. The project team comes and goes leaving the manager with a new system but also an entirely new set of problems and a smaller workforce to deal with them. Does the manager feel any sense of control over what was done to them?

In contrast, where there is true ownership, the manager is involved from the beginning and has a continual say in the design of the new facilities and how they are to be installed so that by the time of implementation they are effectively in charge.

So easy to say. So hard to make happen. Why do managers fall into the 'typical scenario' trap? Sometimes it's due to lack of interest – "let the experts sort it out". Sometimes it's due to inexperience – "it's safer to keep me out of this". Often it's simply a lack of time – "when you're driving at high speed there's no time to think about changing the wheel".

There are no magic bullets here – different situations demand different solutions. What is needed, however, is a clear recognition by both the initiators and receivers of organisation changes that somehow or other ownership must be transferred and the sooner this is talked about the better.

On side's better than off side

It's one of those areas of management where we think we know it all but discover that in fact we don't. I can still remember an external consultant who was advising my change programme coming in one day and asking some simple questions: Who are the big cheeses? Who doesn't believe in what you're doing? Who might do most damage? The questions are all obvious but they're not often asked.

I suppose one assumes that, having heard the CEO giving his support to the programme, everyone will tow the line. Failing that, there is always the old boy network to call on.

If you're involved in organisation change you need to understand your stakeholders and work out who has got most to gain and, conversely, most to lose from what's being proposed. It's also important to identify those individuals who are most able to influence the eventual outcome.

If you're lucky, some of those with most to gain will have powerful positions and be able to help open doors and bend ears. If you're unlucky, the power will lie with those who are at best neutral and at worst in opposition.

It's then all about communicating with the key stakeholders and keeping them 'on side'. Here there is only one rule – remember that everyone is different and needs a different approach. Some people like written reports; some like face-to-face meetings. Some need weekly reminders of progress; for some, 2-monthly updates are sufficient. Some rely entirely on advisors particularly when technology is involved; some make their own judgments.

However you do it, good stakeholder management can make a huge difference to the eventual outcome, so don't undercook it.

Change champions

You'll know them if you've got any working for you. They're the ones who're always coming up with bright ideas about how to do things differently when you really want them to be concentrating on the job at hand. Eventually, if they're ignored too often, they retreat into their shells and apply their enthusiasm outside the workplace.

It's worth cultivating people like this because when your organisation is going through major change they can be a huge asset acting as 'bridges' between those who are responsible for what's changing and those on the receiving end. I call them 'change champions', as the best are out on the front line waving the flag and persuading their colleagues that the water's not as cold as it looks.

Change champions come in all shapes and sizes. They are often in relatively junior jobs and have limited experience but they have some characteristics which make them invaluable:

- They are interested not only in the work to be done but also how it is being done and whether it's being done as smartly and as efficiently as possible.

- They are respected and listened to by their colleagues because they tell things 'like it is' and generally aren't trying to score points or feed personal ambition.

- They have enormous energy and a determination to see things through whatever it takes, regardless of personal cost.

So when you've nothing better to do cast your mind over all your people, make a mental note of all the potential change champions and keep them sweet!

Making use of networks

We all know they're there and yet we don't talk about them. We all have them and indeed would be lost without them but we don't treat them as part of our official armoury. I'm talking about personal networks – one of the most underrated assets possessed by any organisation.

They come in many shapes and sizes – old school chums, drinking mates, fellow joiners or simply like-minded colleagues. By the ambitious they're exploited mercilessly; for the rest of us they're a useful 'support mechanism' to get us through life's ups and downs.

If, however, you're in the business of changing things, networks can be very useful, indeed invaluable, tools:

- as a means of finding out what's actually happening and how things really work. It helps here if you've been clever to scatter your friends widely.

- to help you test out your pet theories without word getting back to 'management'. In some organisations peer reviews are mandatory.

- to provide moral support and act as 'flag bearers' when things start to happen.

- to give honest feedback especially when things go wrong as they inevitably will.

People like being consulted and being asked to give advice. It makes them feel good and gives them the license to return the favour. So don't hold back. Get out there and exploit your networks for all their worth.

Low hurdles

Changing anything in an organisation involves risk. Whether you're changing the work people are doing or the way they go about it (the processes, systems, etc.), there is always a risk that things will go wrong and the enterprise will suffer. Of all the various techniques for managing risk, the method that I've found consistently most useful is to break things down into bite-sized chunks. What were high hurdles are replaced by 'low hurdles' thereby reducing the overall exposure.

This approach, however, often doesn't come naturally. It's easy to picture where you're trying to get to, the final destination. It's much less easy to plot a course involving sometimes dozens of separate changes with difficult transitions between each. It can always be done, though, either by subdividing what it is you're changing, for example dividing the new process into components, or by subdividing the receiving population, for example implementing the change team by team.

Going for low hurdles has two obvious disadvantages. Firstly, it inevitably creates a bigger beast to manage with all that that entails. Secondly, there's likely to be more pressure from top management looking for an early return on investment. To be told that a two year change programme needs to take three "as we need to do a multi-stage implementation" may not go down too well.

So if you contemplate such a course, be prepared for a fight, but stick to your guns. My golden rule on such occasions is to ask what people will remember ten years down the line. Will they remember that the implementation was in spring 2008 rather than autumn 2007 or will they remember that it was an almighty xxxx-up? The choice is yours.

Part 6

Strategy

Value drivers

One of the most important concepts in the armoury of the strategic thinker is that of 'value drivers' – those levers which when pulled most influence the value created by the enterprise for the customer and, where appropriate, for the shareholder.

Value drivers vary depending on the industry, the competitive situation and in-house capabilities. In the consumer products sector, for example, they might relate to the way the organisation deals with the customer, the nature of the products being offered or the way the enterprise operates. Examples of each would be Amazon's customer reviews, Nike's brand and Wal-Mart's supply systems – in every case a critical differentiating factor.

Understanding an enterprise's key value drivers and then going on to measure and manage them is, I would argue, essential to keeping in front of one's competitors – the ultimate source of value.

The beauty of value drivers is that they provide a practical means of turning strategy into action. It is hard work getting people to agree on what they are – often involving the removal of numerous sacrificial cows. Once defined, however, they provide an excellent bridge into the harder job of delivering the results.

People need to know what's important, what will make a difference and what they should focus their efforts upon. Value drivers provide the key.

Future back

There are times when organisations, just like people, realise that the only way forward is by taking a big leap. Incremental changes have run their course and it's time to jump out of the comfort zone and confront the unknown. The problem we all face here is how to shake off all the 'baggage' associated with the way we currently view the world. Organisations, like people, have stacks of unwritten assumptions about what can and can't be done, all of which hold back creative thinking.

The most important lesson I've learned is to move from a 'today forward' approach to thinking 'future back'. Start by painting a picture of how you see the world and the enterprise say 10 years out. Then write down what it would take to get there, what ideas and assumptions will need to be tested, what organisational changes will be required and what funds and talent will be needed. Finally start building a step-by-step plan which gradually converges towards the end point vision.

The process can be described in a few words but it is desperately difficult in practice and many organisations fail for a number of reasons:

- The end point vision is not properly 'grounded' – i.e. the full implications aren't thought through.

- The plan to get there is poorly constructed or focuses solely on the first few steps.

- The vision and plan are not 'bought into' by the stakeholders both inside and outside the organisation.

What's really important is the need for courage. It took Kennedy huge courage to shoot for the moon. From time to time as leaders and managers we need to display similar courage.

Changing strategy

I may be showing my age, but I come from the school that says enterprises need some deep stakes in the ground if they are to survive in this increasingly volatile world. The most important of these is a description of the organisation's long-term objectives, what it aims to be and to do – i.e. its strategy. I don't go with the view that things change so fast that strategy is irrelevant – at any one time people both inside and outside the enterprise need to know what it's about and what it's trying to achieve.

The problem comes when a strategy has to change. There's lots of top level thinking, new ideas emerge, new concepts are tested, full scale pilots are launched and at a critical moment, assuming things are successful, the new strategy is launched. Choosing that moment and moving from strategy development to strategy implementation is one of the hardest leadership decisions there is requiring determination, foresight and a lot of luck.

What's really important is recognising that there is a decision to make. It's simply not good enough to slide gently from small-scale trialling to large-scale roll-out without serious thinking. To commit large amounts of people and money to a new idea is a big issue which cannot be taken lightly.

So next time you observe a change of direction in your enterprise ask a few simple questions. Is this major or minor? If it's major, how was the decision made and when was the decision made? Don't hold your breath waiting for an answer.

Strategy v. capability

Have you noticed that management books tend to fall into one of two types? They either talk about the sexy stuff (markets, products and customers), or the boring stuff (processes, systems and people). They're either interested in an organisation's strategy or its capability.

Top management teams for various reasons are often more comfortable when talking about strategy than capability and this tends to be reflected in the time spent discussing each.

Perhaps it's because of a macho belief that "if we get everybody excited and mobilised we're bound to succeed" whatever our inherent strengths. Perhaps it's because understanding and describing people and processes is seriously difficult and "best left to experts". Perhaps it's because changing the way an organisation operates is a multi-year task compared to the weeks or months required to begin implementing a new strategy.

Whatever the reason, I would argue that a good strategy is worthless unless it is effectively implemented, and this depends critically on the organization's capability.

It's worth speculating on what things might feel like if capability received more attention.

Firstly, there would be robust arguments about how best to organise things, who does what, who reports to whom and how decisions are to be made. Secondly, there would be endless debates about people – have we got the right skills and in the right quantities? If not, when will we have? Finally, there would be hard-nosed sessions with the CIO getting him to explain exactly what the new systems will bring, what risks they entail and what the impact will be on staff.

The very best public and private organisations routinely have such discussions and are comfortable having them. Does yours?

Part 7

Leadership

Goals, objectives and targets

It's a platitude to say that in any enterprise people need to know where they are going. But ask ten employees what the organisation is trying to achieve and I'll bet you get ten different answers. Some will talk about aspirations and some about hard financials. Some will talk long-term and some short. Some will talk globally and some parochially.

So, if you are leading such an enterprise, does this matter? The evidence suggests that it does and the really successful organisations make sure that everyone is pointing, both logically and emotionally, in the same direction all the time.

For all the talk about the increasing rate of global change any organisation can create and maintain a clear forward view of where it's going. By so doing it should always be possible to articulate three things:

- the long term strategy and strategic goals for the enterprise, e.g. £3 billion sales by the start of the next decade.

- medium term objectives, e.g. opening up in Eastern Europe in three years.

- short term targets, e.g. profit growth of 2% this year.

What is more, people need to understand the underpinning rationale and, most importantly, understand the logic behind any changes. Nothing creates distrust in leadership faster than frequent and unexplained changes of direction. Of course, the odd 'course correction' may be necessary but a routine rewriting of the strategic plan gives nobody any confidence.

Being seen when it matters

Many of us were brought up with the image of Henry V at the front of his troops at Agincourt leading the charge. A more recent leadership model is that of the executive being seen everywhere 'walking the talk'. Both techniques are about achieving visibility. Both however can backfire, in the case of the former by producing lousy oratory, in the case of the latter, by interfering rather than simply listening and advising.

Surely what is important is for the leader to be seen when it matters. Most of the time the troops, if well chosen and well managed, will operate happily knowing someone is there in the background pulling the strings. There are times, however, when intervention from the top is needed:

- when something major is about to happen and people need to hear the words of encouragement particularly if extra effort or risk is involved (the Agincourt scenario).

- when a crisis of some sort has just happened and people want to know how best to react – Tony Blair's words after Princess Diana's death stand out here.

- when the organisation is going through a prolonged period of uncertainty and repeated reassurances are needed that things are still on track in spite of possible evidence to the contrary – Churchill's wartime speeches for example.

Deciding, as leader, when to be seen is much more important than deciding how best to appear (in person, on screen, etc.). It's the being there at the critical times which counts the most. I am reminded of the interview of Macmillan in which he was asked what was the hardest thing about being Prime Minister – after a short pause came the reply, 'Events, dear boy, events.'

Short agendas

In the early days of microcomputers a frequently observed phenomenon was that of 'thrashing' – where the computer was so overloaded with jobs it couldn't decide what to do next and stopped working. People experience thrashing; so do organisations, usually because their to-do lists or 'agendas' are too long.

As Pascal observed when commenting on letter-writing, it is often easier to make things long than short. For organisations, particularly organisations in trouble, creating a short list of priorities can be exceptionally hard, but without it people don't know what to focus on and the organisation loses its way.

A useful prioritisation technique is to look at the organisation's activities under three headings:

1. What's needed to keep things going – all the day-to-day essentials to stay alive.

2. What needs to change in the way things are done – people, working practices, systems, etc.

3. What developmental seeds need to be sown for the long term – new markets, new products or new customers.

Under each heading, the question is then "What needs to be done now and what can wait till next year?" For multi-year projects, usually the biggest prioritisation challenge, the clever approach, is to divide into self-contained pieces and then choose a sensible and safe implementation sequence.

In the best run organisations everyone knows "what we've got to do this year" because the agenda is short and has been stated clearly and precisely. There may be a different agenda next year but that's a problem for the leaders not those at the coalface.

Applying good incentives

Leaders have many tools at their disposal, some more powerful than others. Of these one of the most badly used is that of financial incentives which can absorb huge amounts of management time in the devising with little, if any, subsequent pay-off in terms of performance.

So what's going on here? My observation is that most debate surrounds the measures underpinning targets – sales, profit, costs, quality, etc. – and the numerical targets themselves. Much less debate surrounds the way these should be applied to the organisation – whether they are to incentivise individuals, teams or the organisation as a whole.

The difficulty with the latter is that it gets into the thorny but important question of culture and behaviour:

- If you want everybody to work together then go for organisation-wide targets; don't set up incentives that favour some groups over others.

- If you're trying to encourage individual initiative then make it worth peoples' while to go out on a limb.

- If it's teamwork that's needed then set targets for teams as a whole but not the individuals within them.

While these are clearly difficult judgements, the benefits, if well handled, can be huge.

Some years ago, I observed a seemingly endless debate between a manufacturer and wholesaler about how best to reduce internal costs. The argument stopped literally overnight when somebody said "why don't we go for a *joint* cost reduction target!"

Making your mark early

A challenge that all of us have to face from time to time, some more frequently than others, is how to cope with the often exaggerated expectations of the world at large when starting a new job. There's been the build-up of the job announcement and everyone's watching and waiting to see whether you're an improvement over the previous incumbent and how quickly you'll put your foot in it.

The most useful new job technique I know is to pretend that the first 3 months are a probationary period. Talk to everyone, act dumb, ask all the silly naïve questions, and remember that no one will blame you for anything. With luck no great crises will occur leaving plenty of time just to observe and listen, with the box of Kleenex at the ready.

I'm very suspicious of those who leap into action with quick decisions or pronouncements. Whatever prior researches have been done before taking up the position, things are never the same when you talk to people on the ground and understand what's really going on.

Quick action may be what the outside world is expecting but it rarely cuts any ice with those who are looking for leadership. Much better in my experience is to get the people issues sorted early (however trivial), and thereby establish credibility as someone who listens and can be trusted.

If you're determined to do something, then I suggest you follow the advice given by one of my early bosses. His instruction was: soon after taking on a new job, do something "highly visible but totally inconsequential" like painting the office walls a different colour!

Leadership is being consistent

The books on leadership are full of lots of exciting talk about how to be an inspirational leader and lead from the front – i.e. how to motivate your people. It's a great place to start, but to be successful over the long term leaders need to demonstrate a much more boring virtue, that of consistency.

From my observations people soon see through the sexy stuff. When the hype has worn off, what they are looking for is someone who talks and behaves predictably. That way they know where they stand and can get on with the job without forever looking over their shoulder.

Consistency comes in many forms. It starts with consistency of message. Whatever is really important now can't suddenly become unimportant tomorrow. It can't be "sales" today and "costs" tomorrow. Priorities will change but there need to be some 'commandments' which are there for the duration.

Consistency of execution also needs to be visible. Unless there are extremely good reasons things started should be finished even if this takes years. A 'Grand old Duke of York' approach wins no friends.

Finally, and perhaps most importantly of all, a leader needs to show consistency of behaviour. People take their cue as much from the way things are said as from what is said. As a leader whether you're a bully or a charmer probably doesn't matter as long as you behave in the same way each day!

Writing things down

A clever request when visiting a new organisation is to ask to see what's 'written down' – the objectives, the targets and the working practices which have been laid down, agreed and communicated to the workforce. Having such 'rules of engagement' is a visible sign that everyone is going in the same direction, and that there is good leadership around the place.

To be effective the rules of engagement must be comprehensive, clear, useable and consistent:

*   They need to cover both what the organisation is trying to achieve (its strategy, its markets, its goals, etc.) and how people should behave.

*   They need to be written in language that everyone can understand including those at the front line.

*   They must be easy to turn into action – this may mean more detail not less. Wishy-washy principles and mission statements are often a complete waste of time.

*   They must be consistent over time – once written down they must remain valid and in place for years not months.

Doing the writing is a real test for the leaders of an organisation as it quickly exposes gaps in thinking and disagreements between individuals. But the effort is worthwhile.

Many years ago while visiting Wal-Mart's headquarters in Bentonville, Arkansas, I met a young computer programmer who'd only been employed by the company for a few weeks. She pointed to a chart on the corridor wall and proceeded to give me a detailed explanation of the company's targets for that year. Now that shows the power of writing things down!

Having fun

When I cast my mind back through the jobs I've done over the years I remember some as successes, some as failures, but some, the ones I can recall best, stand out from the rest as having been great fun. To quote the hackneyed phrase "we worked hard and played hard".

It's hard to analyse what it is that makes a job fun. There's something magical in the atmosphere that ensures that whatever battles take place during the working day people regard each other as best mates when it's going home time. What's more they often still feel they're best mates ten years on even if they've long been parted.

I am very suspicious of those who say that somehow fun can be imposed. There are of course lots of standard techniques – weekly pub lunches, staff parties and Christmas entertainments come to mind. Maybe I'm getting past it, but I would argue that people take their cue not from what happens out of work time, but what happens in it.

There can never be fun if there is also fear and mistrust. The leaders who preside over people having fun are those who are able to make their staff feel comfortable while at work. They do this in a variety of ways but mainly by making everyone feel that the enterprise has a clear goal, that individual contributions are valuable and appreciated and by treating everyone with respect.

Once people are comfortable at their workplace the fun arises spontaneously. It doesn't have to be forced.

The essence of leadership

"Leaders are born not made." "He'll always be a no.2 never a no. 1." "Management is one thing, leadership quite another."

We've created this image of leadership which suggests that it is something that only a few can aspire to. My view is that many of us have the capability to be good leaders. Whether we choose to be leaders is another matter entirely.

For me the essence of leadership rests in two words: inspiration and trust – inspiring people to follow you, and giving them the confidence that you can be trusted to lead them in the right direction.

Inspiration is all about building an exciting and believable vision of where you're trying to get to. Whatever the task people must be emotionally committed – this will only happen if you take time out for 'picture painting'.

Building trust is orders of magnitude harder and comes about through deeds and not through words by:

- delivering on your promises unless there are very good reasons for not doing so.

- being consistent over time – nobody trusts someone who forever changes course .

- treating people with respect, rewarding the heroes, picking up the losers and never 'messing anyone around'.

If you think back through your career you'll recall leaders who inspired you whom you didn't trust and some whom you trusted but weren't inspiring. Those who did both will have left a permanent rosy glow that should never be extinguished.

Part 8

Information Technology

Thinking about IT (1)

It is now 50 years since computers were first used in business. In that time we have seen a move from 'data processing' to 'information management' with the internet as the latest manifestation of the latter. Whereas once the computer (the only one) was hidden away in a secret machine room, today every desktop has one.

In spite of such extraordinary developments I would contend that when thinking about IT we should still ask the same basic questions that we asked when I was a lad punching IBM Assembler programs into 80 column cards.

1. Are we clear about the business problem we're trying to solve? Is it to increase sales, increase margin or decrease operating costs?

2. Have we thought about how things should ideally work – the operating processes – and what it will require of people to operate these processes?

3. Do we know why people want information? Is it to identify and then act on poor performance? Is it to help make investment decisions? Is it to spot trends? Is it simply to keep up to date?

4. Do the new systems provide a catalyst to enable more profound changes to take place?

The technologies may have changed. The questions haven't.

System prototypes

Engineers and construction workers are never happier than when the detailed drawing has been signed off by the client and they are left in peace to get on with the job. Software builders are of a similar breed – tell them what the system has to do and they'll happily work away in isolation until the day on which the covers are taken off and you discover that it either doesn't do what you expected or it does but takes your people ages to learn.

It's partly a communication issue. Getting a 'techie' to explain things is never easy. More often it's a project management issue. When the software builders are up against tight deadlines the last thing they want is to take time out having long debates about how the system 'looks and feels'.

The best solution to this problem is to make use of system 'prototypes' which look and feel like the real thing but behind the covers don't do a lot. So if you're expecting a sales information system get the software writers early on to put together a series of screen shots showing real data and tell them to go away while you and your people think about what you've got and whether it will do the job. By setting up a continuing dialogue like this there is a much better chance of a successful outcome.

The over 40s among us still find operating the video remote control a nightmare. If the designers of these devices had done some prototyping perhaps we'd find the buttons we use the most in bright colours, extra large and at the top of the box!

Information for decision-making

How often do you find yourself saying "I feel sure I could make better decisions with better information? Why can't the IT people sort something out?" Well, I've been an IT person and I can tell you that providing good information for decision-makers has always been the biggest challenge for the IT professional.

Why is it so hard?

The main reason is that most managers find it very difficult to describe their jobs in the detail needed by the IT professional. "I'm responsible for selecting locations for new retail stores and need to know everything about the catchments and the offers we could mount." Try turning that into an easily useable information system.

The converse situation also arises when new information becomes available and the problem is how to capitalise on it. The classic example in retailing is the data collected on individual customer purchases when they use loyalty cards.

With new information such as this, managers don't know what to do with it. They don't know what decisions they could make and need help. Here the only way forward for the manager and his IT colleague is to do joint research into how best to exploit this new capability for the organisation's benefit.

Whatever the reason, with problems as hard as this the only solution is dialogue. Only by working closely together can the information user and the information provider make the information delivered match the decisions to be made.

Thinking about IT (2)

In the early 90s the business press talked endlessly about using IT to 'reengineer' corporations and make them fitter and leaner. Ten years on, having seen a number of resulting failures, people are much more sober about how IT can actually be made to work to benefit the organisation. And this is in spite of vastly increased technology capability. So what's going on here?

The fact is that designing and implementing new systems has become much harder than it was in the 'glory days' of the 70s and 80s. Whereas once it was a question of automating relatively self-contained operations (order processing, payroll, etc.), now whole swathes of interconnected activities can be involved, such is the power of IT. Indeed the phrase 'enterprise computing' is now in common use.

Things are made even harder in that the old rule about designing new processes first and then fitting the technology doesn't work when you're buying a ready-made system package into which the software manufacturer has built what he believes is the best way of doing things – so called 'industry best practice'.

But the final challenge is the most difficult to handle. People have now woken up and are demanding that their wants and needs are taken into account when new systems are introduced. In other words we need to think about the way IT affects the 'soft stuff' – competencies and behaviours – as well as the hard stuff.

Technology as catalyst

They may not realise it but the IT people in an organisation are highly privileged. Because of what they do they have a unique perspective on the way the organisation works and how it could work better. What is more, by thinking about and then applying technology they can act as 'catalysts' bringing about long overdue changes.

This can happen in several ways.

Firstly, IT can provide reliable information on what is actually happening, thus allowing a move away from 'management by anecdote' – consider the transition that took place, for example, when retailers introduced point-of-sale systems in the late 80s and discovered that what they were selling wasn't what they had thought.

The second catalytic effect started to occur when communications technology appeared and has mushroomed with the internet. Here we are talking about enterprises suddenly able to behave as if both their employees and their trading partners operated out of a single room. A good current example is Ebay which was inconceivable prior to the internet.

Perhaps the most profound impact of technology occurs simply because of the need when introducing systems to document the surrounding activities and introduce so-called 'process disciplines'. The apparently simple act of writing down who's actually responsible for something, and by implication who's not, can clear up years of confusion, and all because the IT man wants to put in a new system.

Thinking about IT (3)

I describe it as that ghastly moment when the scales fall off the eyes and the full implications of putting in this new system become clear. It's when the project leader says "We need to understand your processes and decide how they need to change." The air suddenly turns chill. What's all this about? What's he talking about? I haven't a clue what our processes are – we just do things, we don't have processes.

As the receiving manager you're about to cross a Rubicon – from that moment on you will have worry not only about what work has to be done by your people but also about how it is carried out. History is littered with IT implementation failures all resulting from not thinking clearly enough about how, at the grass roots level, the nature of work has to change.

At the end of the day you and your team will need to ask three big questions:

1.   Do we understand how our people do their jobs now? Don't say it's all in the operating manuals – these are rarely used.

2.   Are we clear about how best to operate when the new system is installed? Have we taken enough time to understand what will be possible, how things can be simplified, what tasks will disappear, and what impact there will be on our people?

3.   Have we thought how to ensure that the new processes are followed week in week out? New systems are usually quite 'intolerant' and require people to follow rules.

Big questions, but once answered you can focus on what's really important – leading your people through the change.

Loosely coupled systems

When you've been involved in installing large computer systems over a long period you learn a few hard lessons which are not written in the textbooks. Of these the one I've found most useful is that of 'loose coupling' – i.e. keeping different systems at arms' length from each other.

So, for example, if you've got computerised tills in shops passing sales data to a head office sales reporting system you make sure that when one till breaks down the sales reports keep coming out albeit without that till's data.

This may seem obvious, but with ever faster computers and communications networks the trend is towards vast 'enterprise systems' which do everything and in which all the separate pieces 'talk to each other' constantly.

Why go for loosely coupled systems? Two reasons: they're easier to implement and safer to operate. By keeping the pieces separate it means that software development can be split across different teams and that implementation can be easily phased, thus avoiding the dreaded 'big bang' effect.

Once the systems are up and running, the handling of failures is easier as the faulty pieces can easily be isolated, like sealing off the damaged sections of a torpedoed submarine.

All this does, however, come at a price. It requires up front some extremely clear thinking about the overall systems 'architecture' so that when everything's finally in place the pieces work together. But the long-term pay-off will be substantial.

Justifying IT

Thinking about IT and its contribution to an enterprise in the 21st century is much harder than when it all began in the 1950s. In those days, the case for IT investment was straightforward – we were replacing data processing by people with data processing by electronic computers, and the justification was based on hours saved.

Today IT is pervasive. It is everywhere, from the executive suite to the shop floor and yet we still try to put both IT development and the case for investing in IT in a box labelled "for the attention of the Chief Information Officer only". The one remaining argument for such an approach is that, whether we like it or not, IT sometimes has to be implemented in big bundles, for example when putting in large 'enterprise systems' such as SAP.

50 years on from the start of all this, I suggest it is time to move on. Of course we still need central management of data and the imposition of technology standards but, apart from this, shouldn't we expect all managers to take the initiative, get to know what's possible and make their own case for IT investment? If they choose to ignore potential opportunities they will lose out in the marketplace and lose the support of their staff who want the best tools to do the job.

Remember – everyone under 25 has known nothing else since birth.

Secrets of IT success

We all know that IT projects, particularly big IT projects, are risky, and yet we know also that many succeed – these get much less publicity than the failures. So what makes the difference? What are the distinguishing features of successful IT projects?

For me it all boils down to four things.

Firstly, the technology must be proven. It's fine being the first company to use this system or the first to use it in this way, but you need to be sure that the underlying mechanics, whether software or hardware, work reliably and at sufficient speed (this is still important).

Secondly, the business requirement must be fully understood. This means being crystal clear how people will work with the new facilities and information and also how the same people will make the transition from where they are now to where they will end up.

Thirdly, the overall project management must be a joint responsibility between the deliverers (the IT and process people) and the receivers (those managers and staff affected). If there is even a paper-thin crack between the two groups, things will inevitably go wrong.

Finally, the new 'system disciplines' – technical support, data maintenance and process compliance – need to be properly trained in and operating from day one.

Sort out the basics and you'll be on track to succeed.

Part 9

Management General

Projects v. processes

Have you ever wondered why some people completely collapse after a job move which on the surface should be well within their capability? A common explanation is that they've made a switch from managing 'projects' to managing 'processes' – from activities which have a timescale and a definite deliverable to activities which are about line management such as running a marketing department or product buying.

The differences between the two types of management are profound but rarely understood as they are much more about style than about skill:

- Successful project managers are all instinctive planners – they don't have to have critical paths, resource variances or 'checkpoints' explained. These come naturally.

- The best process managers are brilliant at juggling competing priorities and thrive on pressure. They go cold however when faced with an empty diary and a blank sheet of paper.

- Feelings of achievement are different. For the project manager the best days are uneventful with the plan on schedule and all the key issues under control. The process manager, on the other hand, is happiest when dozens of crises have been resolved and customers have gone away happy.

In my career I haven't come upon many people capable of both types of management. It's critical therefore when redesigning organisations, appointing people to jobs or simply assigning tasks, to recognise that we are talking about oil and water here – project and process skills don't mix.

Managing or leading?

There are lots of books on management and there are lots of different books on leadership. So if you're a 'team leader' responsible for managing a large project, which type of book do you buy? For many of us, this is a daft distinction which implies that managing people is a specialist task for leaders only.

It doesn't matter whether it's a large department, a complex project or a small team that you're managing. The toughest management challenges are always to do with people, and leadership skills in one form or another are bound to be needed.

It's worth asking why we think of management and leadership separately. I would suggest that for most aspects of management there are rules and processes that can be written down (how to manage projects, how to manage accounts, etc.), and these can be taught.

When it comes to people the text books only take you so far. I defy anyone to write an instruction book on how to go about inspiring your people. This is 'woolly stuff' and therefore often regarded as dangerous and best left to leadership gurus.

Not all managers can be top-level inspirational leaders. All managers can and should, however, take the time to learn the basics about leadership and thereby ensure that that the people they're managing give of their very best.

Midpoint measures

"What you can't measure you can't manage," while somewhat hackneyed, still holds a lot of truth. The trouble is, what precisely do you measure and how do you deal with the results? I have seen countless hours wasted on constructing elaborate measurement systems that weren't properly thought through and hence were never effectively used.

The quick answer is to measure the results – sales, customer satisfaction, factory output, etc. While obviously necessary, these cannot be sufficient as the reasons for over or under-performance may at best be apocryphal without some underlying measures in place.

The clever thing is to define a set of 'midpoint' measures which act as a halfway house between the outputs you are trying to achieve and the root factors determining these outputs – product quality, customer awareness, etc. By tracking such midpoint measures you can look 'upwards' to their effects and 'downwards' to their causes.

In manufacturing my favourite midpoint measure is production schedule adherence. If people keep to plan, the outputs will be achieved and costs minimised. By analysing poor schedule adherence the causes of low output will be understood.

Once a set of midpoint measures has been defined and targets set, achieving these can be the focus for many managers. The rule becomes, "Achieve your targets and the results will follow."

Minimal frameworks – management in 30 seconds

The best lesson in management I've ever read appeared in a little book on 'work design'. It said that people should be given a minimal specification of what's wanted and then left to get on with it.

Two things are important here: first, that a specification is needed – by this the author meant something clearly written down, not some vague instructions; second, that this should be minimal – it should provide the widest possible degrees of freedom to individuals to optimise their talents (in today's jargon provide 'empowerment').

For a 30-second course in management, this can't be beaten. A 'framework' approach can be applied to everything that needs to be managed – the strategy, the products and services, the targets, the plans and the rules of behaviour. For each of these the question should be, "What must we lay down in blocks of stone and what can we leave to individuals' intelligence?"

Getting this right is no mean feat – it requires a lot of extremely clear thinking and great moral courage. What is often surprising is how little rather than how much needs to be written down – but what is written down has to be right.

If you look at most really successful organisations you will find minimal frameworks in one form or another. Why? Because top leaders know that there is no better way to get the best from their people.

Thick-skinned v. thin-skinned

Some of the most confusing, frustrating and enervating people problems arise from the interaction between thick and thin-skinned individuals. Understanding this can save a lot of management time and associated grief.

Thick-skinned individuals tend to assume that others are similarly inclined and therefore able to take the rough stuff. Thin-skinned individuals assume that others are sensitive and should be treated with a tender touch.

Nowhere is the problem more apparent than when one is boss and the other subordinate.

When thick-skinned Joe supervises thin-skinned Nigel, it is all highs or lows. When things go well Nigel is in cloud nine, overwhelmed by the praise. When things go badly he wants to slit his wrists so pained is he with the rough criticism from his boss.

When it's the reverse things are much more complex and confusing. When thin-skinned Nigel supervises thick-skinned Joe, everything in the latter's eyes is underplayed – praise is mealy-mouthed and criticisms wimpish and barely noticed. Nigel, meanwhile, doesn't understand how to get through to his subordinate so afraid is he to fire the necessary 'exocets'.

Lesson: take time out to reflect on the relative sensitivities of the people around you – it may explain some of the frustrations you observe in their relationships.

The three types of management

We all have our pet theories about top-level management. One of my personal favourites is that when you strip things right back it comes in three (and only three) types:

- management of stable businesses

- management of rapidly changing businesses

- management of new or fledgling businesses.

Each type requires distinctive managerial skills, processes and behaviours and, most importantly, there is not much overlap.

Stable businesses need well established targets, people incentivised to achieve those targets and constant monitoring of the external environment to ensure that complacency doesn't set in.

Changing businesses (e.g. businesses being 'downsized') need exceptional focus on what has to be done by when, on the planning of people's time and on the control of risks.

New or fledgling businesses need plenty of 'space' to encourage creativity – i.e. a light touch but, at the same time, tight control of the release of funds.

Two key implications: firstly, large enterprises may have to cope with all three types of business under the same roof and hence have to treat them differently; secondly, when a business moves from one type to another, for example when a new business stabilises, the leaders may have to change also.

FLEDGLING BUSINESS

RAPIDLY CHANGING BUSINESS

STABLE BUSINESS

Sensitively using sensitivities

It's the end of a long session in which a colleague has just explained how his new idea will revolutionize the business and lead to that upturn that everyone's waiting for. All he wants is for the management team to sign up and write the necessary cheque. And yet deep down you feel that it won't go so smoothly, but can't find a way of saying so without sounding negative.

In such circumstances, the most useful technique I know is to ask about 'sensitivities' – i.e. how sensitive the final result is to each of the underlying assumptions, and how much the final result will change as each underlying assumption is varied.

So if the proposal is to introduce a shop in a new location, the business case will make assumptions about the numbers of potential customers, their individual spending power, their price expectations, the reactions of competitors, etc. For each of these the question should be "what if?" What if the customer numbers are 10% less than you forecast? What if they each spend 20% less than you predict?

But sensitivities can have an upside as well as a downside. I have seen new projects fail because people weren't bold enough and didn't move fast enough. Here the question might be, "If we gave you twice as much money and you were able to halve the timescales what difference would this make to the value of the project?"

Whether it's a downside or upside discussion, the point is that by quantifying causes and effects over-exuberant optimism and under-exuberant pessimism can each be replaced by a realistic approach in which both the heart and the head play a part.

Managing externals v. managing internals

A recent trend has seen the move across industry sectors to outsourcing of whole functions, IT being the most common. While subcontracting has been around for some time it is only relatively recently that the phenomenon has become widespread. This raises the obvious question – do the management techniques that I've successfully used for years with internal staff apply when I'm dealing with people who've been outsourced?

My answer would be 'yes and no'. Yes because all the things that need to be managed – delivery dates, quality, financials, risk, etc. – still need managing. No because the way this is done may be profoundly different when the people belong to a different organisation with different rules, incentives and behavioural norms, all of which create a hidden 'curtain' through which you now have to operate.

So what's the solution? The model that works best for me is to think in terms of 'pinch points' – ways in which activities crossing the organisational boundary can be monitored and if necessary controlled. Pinch points can take several forms:

- service level agreements on both sides defining unambiguously each party's responsibilities and accompanied by high level joint progress reviews

- individuals specifically appointed to act as account or client managers and charged with keeping everyone in line

- joint incentives aimed at ensuring that everyone of whatever organisation points in the same direction.

I could go on but hopefully I've said enough to persuade you to manage your externals with intelligence.

Alternating layers of incompetence

How often have you scratched your head after something's gone seriously wrong and said, "How on earth did that we let that happen? With all our checks and balances it should have been impossible." My observation over the years is that one of the biggest reasons for failure is having the same incompetence at two levels in an organisation – 'the blind leading the blind'.

Pity those who report to a bad people manager whose boss is also a bad people manager. To whom do they turn for help? What a surprise when a financially illiterate manager lets a dud project go ahead when his boss is similarly illiterate. How many new product failures result from marketeer and boss wearing the same rose-tinted spectacles?

Management theory would suggest that with sufficient control processes in place – checkpoints, peer reviews, etc. – an organisation can marginalise most incompetence. In practice, however, most decision-making takes place between individuals. If both have similar weaknesses, then watch out!

The clever solution to this is to make sure that glaring incompetences are covered above and below – i.e. that the layers alternate. If I'm a financial illiterate then I'd better make sure that at least one person in my team, preferably more than one, isn't. If my boss is similarly inclined either one of us should go or we'd better talk about it and soon.

The miracle of milestones

Whenever I've had to run programmes or projects, at some point or other I've had an 'expert' knocking on the door trying to persuade me to use a highly complex reporting system aimed at showing the status of everything that's going on. The work involved in maintaining such a system can be enormous and at the end of the day you find yourself wondering whether all the effort has been worthwhile.

For me, nothing beats the use of milestones – an agreed set of critical dates each of which is tied to a key component to be delivered and for each of which an individual or team can be held responsible. There shouldn't be too many. I'd expect, whatever the size of the programme, only a very few per month. More than that and they're not milestones.

Having such a framework brings several benefits. Firstly, it is an excellent method of communication – everyone understands dates and dates can easily be remembered.

Secondly, it provides a great way of linking together separate strands of activity which are mutually dependent. Milestones, if carefully designed, provide invaluable 'synchronisation' points at which the different streams of work come together.

Finally, and most importantly, if well devised and fully bought into by the workers, milestones provide a superb set of emotional 'hooks' to which people can get attached and thereby fully commit themselves.

Coming up with milestones which are both challenging but realistic is by no means easy and needs a great deal of careful thought and the wisdom of experience. If done well, however, the pay-back can be enormous.

MILESTONE   MILLSTONE

Working with volunteers

Most of us at some stage in our lives succumb to our social consciences and find ourselves sitting amongst school governors, parish councillors or other such worthy groups of volunteers. Those of us who make this leap from the world of paid employment to the world of the unpaid often find it a tremendous shock. Suddenly all those assumptions that you have always taken for granted don't apply:

- People can't be told to do anything. They have to be asked to do things and they may well say no.

- Individual motivations for volunteering may be very different. Trying to instil team behaviour can be difficult if not impossible.

- The 'ticking clocks' of financial year end, contract termination, board commitment, etc., rarely exist. Getting things done fast can therefore present a major challenge.

- Hearts are often far more important than heads when it comes to agreeing a course of action and the accompanying passion can be fierce.

And yet, and yet, the huge success of numerous voluntary organisations bears witness to the fact that things do get done albeit in a different way from what one may be used to.

The main lesson I've learned is to be patient and not expect to be able to make an immediate difference. Many of those management disciplines you've acquired over the years will be applicable in your new environment. Just don't expect it to happen overnight.

The other lesson is that all those 'soft' personnel skills that may be rusty from under-usage will be invaluable in an arena where how you say things is as important as what you say.

Beware of spurious neatness

It's been a longstanding belief of mine that only so much of life can be neat. Life comes in many forms and guises. Trying to impose more neatness than is natural only leads to frustration and grief. Nowhere is this more obvious than when one is talking about people and organisations and the way they interact.

Take as an example one of my bête noirs, the setting of performance targets. You know the story – the company policy is clear: all staff must be given 'smart' targets so that individual performance can be precisely measured and the available bonus money fairly distributed. Well fine, but the members of my team are doing different types of job. Some have clearly quantifiable objectives but some don't. In the desire for management neatness I'll end up penalising some and inappropriately rewarding others.

Take another example, the trend towards 'flat organisational structures' as a way of speeding up decision-making. Where you're talking about frontline operations – sales, production, etc. – it makes a lot of sense to give managers a wide span of control and thereby prevent too much meddling. It doesn't make sense at all in backroom 'thinking' functions such as business development, where complex ideas need endless discussion between managers and their subordinates. Again a push for a neat single solution leads inevitably to distress.

The simple fact is that diversity is all around us and should be treasured. Just because someone high up thinks in neat mental models does not give him or her the right to impose these on everyone else.

Time management

I once had a boss who never in any circumstances looked under pressure. Everyone raced around like lunatics while he sat behind his desk apparently calm and in control, whatever crises were taking place. Whatever he did was unhurried. I found it infuriating and couldn't understand how he pulled it off.

I've since decided that it's a lot to do with time, both how you manage it and how you think about it. It requires both having a sensible forward diary and an ability to concentrate on one thing at a time.

The average manager's diary has back-to-back meetings with little space left over for anything else. Any kind of thinking gets pushed to the evening or worse the weekend.

You have to ask a few questions here. Does everything have to be done by people in groups? Are individuals unable to work solo or do they simply want to look busy? How come all meetings last exactly 30, 60, or 90 minutes? Is this an amazing law of nature?

The second issue, how you think about time, is much deeper but in the end much more important. The greatest feat of all is to learn to switch on to each new task, concentrate fiercely while it's going on and then completely switch off at the end. By creating a thought free moment at the end of each meeting you bring yourself back to earth and are then ready and able to give your full attention to the next encounter.

What I am describing is not easy but the energy that can thereby be released is enormous. I am reminded of a wonderful quote I once heard from a wise sage*: "It is not a virtue to feel tired at the end of the working day."

* reference to Jagdish Parikh, author of *Managing Your Self*, Blackwell, 1991

Understanding numbers

I'm not normally unkind to accountants but I do feel that the accountants' way of presenting and talking about numbers doesn't always help the difficult task of management. Rightly or wrongly the bookkeeper's desire to document everything to the last penny can create clouds of complexity which makes it difficult at times to see what's actually going on.

Two areas in particular make me mad – spurious accuracy and the use of multiple yardsticks.

The first can occur when looking back but more often is an issue when looking forward. Most backward reporting depends on IT systems which attempt to record what's actually happened. My only gripe here would be that buried within a P&L or balance sheet will be numbers that should be marked with a 'danger' warning due to probable inaccuracy.

Looking forward is a different matter. Here much is 'finger in the air' but you'll see a factory manager confidently predicting future business to the nearest pound when in fact he hasn't a clue what will happen. Why don't we recognise that the future is uncertain and start hedging our bets by using probabilities for example?

My second issue, the use of yardsticks, concerns how we assess the significance of numbers. On one computer report you'll see a product's sales for this week compared simultaneously with sales for last week, the same week last year, the budget, and with sales of comparable products. What is a simple mind supposed to do with this lot?

We should spend more time thinking about why we look at numbers, how to assess their significance and hence how they should be reported. By presenting them selectively and intelligently rather than en masse we could make a huge difference to managers' productivity.

The ultimate survival tool

For some of us it has always come naturally; for others it's a skill we've had to acquire. For some of us it is an essential part of our personal armoury; for others it is a necessary evil. Some of us believe that it should never under any circumstances be used.

I'm talking about 'bullshit', a management tool which is rarely discussed but which is essential for long-term survival in any organisation.

I'm sorry if this is treading on sensitive toes but the simple fact is that if you want your voice to be heard against the clamour of many others a certain amount of overplaying and 'talking the subject up' can be extremely useful.

If you're trying to raise funds for a new opportunity then for goodness sake plug the benefits hard and don't be afraid of some limited overselling. If you've spotted a problem that demands everyone's attention then be prepared to paint a somewhat doom-laden disaster scenario. If it's the annual appraisal and you feel a pay rise is due then a bit of overt personal marketing won't come amiss.

Those of us who've been brought up in disciplines where precision has to be the way of life, engineering, finance and IT for example, often find it difficult to shake off an obsession with accuracy and telling it exactly as it is, no more no less. Whether we like it or not we are surrounded by people for whom this is far from the case and for whom elaboration of the truth is quite normal.

So go on. Be bold. If you've not done it before try applying a few ounces of bullshit every day. It won't hurt and it will help you keep your head above water.

Conclusion

If you've made it this far I assume that some of what you've read has proved interesting and will be useful in the workplace.

As I said at the outset, this book won't tell you everything about management – hopefully, though, it will act as a thought provoker and provide a set of 'hooks' on which to hang your own experiences, learnings and ideas.

If there is one thought I'd like to leave you with it's this: don't ever underestimate the power of people. However awkward the situation or the behaviour of those around you, I would argue that deep down most people most of the time want things to go well. If things don't appear that way it's the fault of management not workers.

If you carry this belief around at all times and keep people and their needs at the front of your mind then you've done all you can.

Best wishes and good luck!

Tony Kemmer

l. 68, 110